TOP DOG

How to Have Fun with Your BFF

Best
Furry
Friend

by Dr. Sophia Yin

Scholastic Inc.

D1710368

To my Best Furry Friend, Jonesy - S.Y.

Illustrations by Lili Chin

Design by Peggy Doody

Cover photos: Jack Russell © AnetaPics / Shutterstock; background © Mila Atkovska / Shutterstock.
All photos of the author © Sophia Yin.
All illustrations © Scholastic except for the following © Sophia Yin: p. 8; p. 10; p. 11; p. 13: top row left and center, bottom row left; p. 14: top row center, middle row center; p. 15: top row left and center; p. 21.

ISBN 978-0-545-58833-1

12 11 10 9 8 7 6 5 4 3 2 1   14 15 16 17 18 19/0
Printed in the U.S.A.   40
First printing, January 2014

Hi there!
I am Dr. Sophia Yin.

I am a veterinarian and an animal behaviorist. I've been studying dogs and their humans for over two decades. And this is Fido. He wants to be your BFF, or Best Furry Friend.

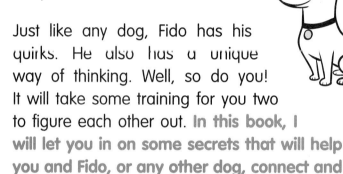

Just like any dog, Fido has his quirks. He also has a unique way of thinking. Well, so do you! It will take some training for you two to figure each other out. In this book, I will let you in on some secrets that will help you and Fido, or any other dog, connect and become best buddies. Let's go!

Contents

Chapter 1

Get to Know Your Best Furry Friend

Most of my friends are dog lovers. Some even say they like their dogs better than their human friends. You might wonder, "How can this be? What is it about Fido that makes him such a great friend?" Here are just a couple of reasons.

Fido Always Has Time for You

Human friends and family are great. But when everyone is too busy to play with you, Fido's not. What if you don't want to play? No problem! When you want to chill out and read a book, Fido's right there to keep you company.

Fido's Friendship Is Steady

Fido loves you whether you made the winning goal for your team—or scored a point for the other team. And if you are wearing funny clothes or having a bad hair day, Fido doesn't care. In fact, no matter what, Fido is always happy to see you! What more could you ask for in a friend?

Of course, a true friendship goes two ways. If you want Fido to be your BFF, you'll have to prove that you can be a pal to him, too. You'll have to learn about what he likes or dislikes, and how he thinks. Let's figure out what makes Fido tick.

Think Like Fido

Fido isn't human. So you can't communicate with him like he's one of your two-legged buddies. To really get through to your BFF, you'll have to keep these basic points in mind.

Fido Doesn't Understand What You're Saying

Then how does he figure you out? Fido's a champ at reading body language. He can read your moods and tell if you're happy or sad. Sometimes he can guess at what you want him to do. But humans can be very confusing to Fido at times. We often tell him to do something, but our bodies signal something else.

Once, someone complained to me about how her dog greeted her. He jumped on her even when she kept telling him "down" and pushing him away. Although she liked that her dog was happy, the jumping got her clothes dirty. One time, he even knocked her down! What was wrong?

Well . . . her dog just didn't understand the meaning of "down." And he thought she was playing with him by pushing him away. He thought that was fun!

If Fido's behavior earns him a reward, then he'll repeat those actions. If his behavior brings him nothing good, then Fido will try to do something else instead.

How did we get "Jumpy" to greet politely? Very simply, we removed the reward for jumping, which is any type of attention. His human avoided talking to him when he rushed over. She stood completely still with her arms folded against her body. Then, when Jumpy eventually sat down, she rewarded him with a treat or petting.

Fido's Many Moods

You just learned about how Fido can read your moods. Now it's your turn to learn his moods. It's always great to know when your BFF is happy. But you also need to recognize when he's scared. This way, you can help protect him.

Fido's Happy Signs

Similar to happy humans, a happy dog is relaxed. Fido will pay attention to the object or person making him happy.

Mouth opens in a smile. It's called an open-mouth play face.

Ears point forward if he is excited.

His tail wags level to his body or higher. Sometimes he will wag in a circle or his entire rear end will wiggle.

Wag Alert!

A wagging tail doesn't always mean a happy dog. It might mean that Fido's excited. Sometimes, this excitement can be caused by happiness. Sometimes, it's not. It can mean that he's on alert for danger. For instance, Fido can wag his tail as he runs to bark at an intruder. When Fido is excited out of fear, he'll usually show signs of nervousness. What are they? Learn about them on the following pages.

You can also tell if Fido likes being petted. He will lean against you as you pet him.

If a dog is nervous or scared, it is sometimes pretty obvious to spot. He'll be cowering—by a little or a lot.

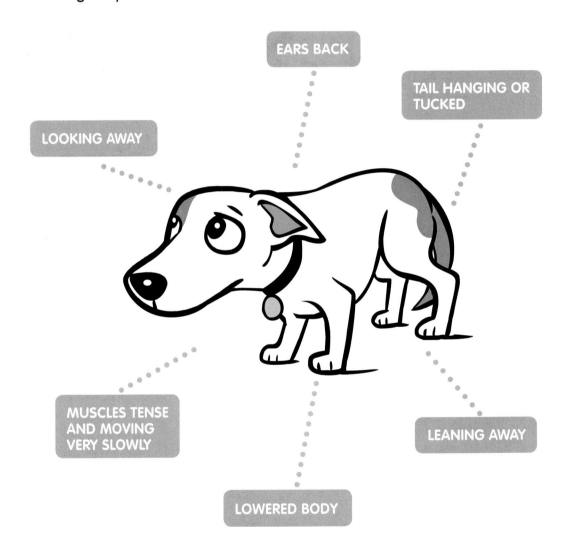

EARS BACK

TAIL HANGING OR TUCKED

LOOKING AWAY

MUSCLES TENSE AND MOVING VERY SLOWLY

LEANING AWAY

LOWERED BODY

Then there are other signs that are not as easy to spot. If Fido shows these signs, he could be anxious.

Sometimes your BFF may pace or pant when he isn't hot or thirsty.

Fido might take short glances in many directions. He's looking for potential danger.

He has a tense facial expression while holding his ears back or out to the side.

Sometimes Fido will just turn away from you and avoid eye contact. He may even lick his lips when no food is nearby.

Last but not least, when Fido is stressed he might show this set of signs: Yawn when he shouldn't be tired; move in slow motion; look or act sleepy. Even if he is hungry, he may lose his appetite.

Chapter 2
Know the No-No's

You now know how to tell when Fido is scared. It's time to learn WHAT makes him scared or unhappy.

Have you ever seen a dog so cute, you just want to run up to him and pet him? This is a nice greeting, right? Unfortunately, to a dog who doesn't know you this may not seem like a friendly move. Instead of making him happy, it may scare him. It may even cause him to feel threatened and try to defend himself. Oops.

How do you greet a dog you don't know very well? Here's an easy answer: Steer clear of the same types of greetings that we humans find scary, rude, or uncomfortable. Let's check them out.

No-No Interactions for Humans and Dogs

You wouldn't do this.   **So don't do that.**   **The Right Approach:**

Reaching into a stranger's car to greet them can scare them.

Fido may feel threatened if you bother him this way. He may even bite.

Stand a safe distance away. This way, Fido doesn't feel threatened.

Rushing up to a stranger can freak them out.

Fido can be just as alarmed.

Take a relaxed walk toward Fido.

You wouldn't do this.   So don't do that.   The Right Approach:

Hugging a stranger without asking for permission can be unwelcome.

This could feel just as scary to Fido.

Be polite and ask to interact with Fido.

Staring at people can make them feel uncomfortable.

It can make Fido feel uneasy, too.

Approach sideways. Look at Fido using peripheral vision instead.

Hovering over someone can make her feel scared.

Fido can get scared when unfamiliar people get too close.

Make sure to stay outside Fido's bubble. Be sure to approach him from the side.

You wouldn't do this.   So don't do that.   The Right Approach:

Sticking out your hand for a stranger to sniff is an invasion of someone's space.

If Fido doesn't know a person well, he might think she's going to grab or hurt him.

Present your side to Fido and let him approach at his own rate. This position will more likely put a dog at ease.

It's not wise to approach someone who looks clearly scared of you.

If Fido looks anxious as you approach, it's best to back off and give him space.

It's OK to pet a dog if he looks relaxed, comes up to you, and rubs against you.

Sometimes people just don't like getting their face pinched.

Some dogs like Fido just don't enjoy overly familiar gestures. Dogs often dislike hugging, kissing, and rough handling.

Pay attention to Fido's feelings and interact in ways that he enjoys.

Don't Be Rude

Great! You now know what NOT to do when greeting a dog. But what are some everyday no-no's? To help keep your BFF happy, don't be rude. You should treat Fido the same way as you want a friend or a family member to treat you.

You wouldn't like it if someone tried to take or play with your food while you were eating.

Fido doesn't like to be bothered during meals either.

You'd be upset if your friend tried to take your game while you were playing with it.

Sometimes, Fido dislikes having his toys stolen or grabbed from him, too.

It's irritating when someone gets into your personal space.

Fido can find this annoying, too.

Being woken up from a comfortable sleep can make anyone grumpy.

That's why it's best to stay away and let a sleeping dog lie.

Loud yelling can get on your nerves.

It can stress your dog out, too. When interacting with Fido, use your inside voice.

No one enjoys having her hair tugged.

Fido also dislikes being tugged and poked.

You wouldn't want someone to trample over you.

This can cause Fido to become scared or agitated.

Chapter 3
Don't Forget to Have Fun

You read about the no-no's. Now it's time to have some fun! Fido loves to play. Here are some simple activities that are fun for both dogs and humans!

Play Fetch!

Many dogs naturally love to chase toys. To start this game, take a ball and throw it. Then see if Fido chases it. If he does, but doesn't yet know to bring it back, toss a second toy. If a ball doesn't do it for him, try a squeaky toy, or some toy that he is already interested in. Show him you have the toy and wave it around. When he looks interested, toss!

Go for a Walk

Dogs love to go on walks! This is great because they need this type of exercise every day. It also helps Fido get used to the sights and sounds around him. You might think that walking is just, well, walking. But there are many games you can play during your walks. You'll learn some in the next chapter. Remember to always bring an adult on your walks. Also, be sure to obey local laws. Keep your BFF on a leash and clean up after him.

Hide-and-Seek

Have a friend hold Fido's collar while you look for a place to hide. Have your friend encourage Fido to watch you. When you have found a good hiding spot, like behind a chair, call Fido. When he finds you, praise and pet him. And then repeat the game. Start with easy hideouts because some dogs don't know to search. Once he knows, you'll be able to make the game more challenging!

Learn with Fido

One of the most fun things you can do with Fido is to train him to do stuff. Before you can do that, you must first learn these important rules.

Rule 1: Remove Rewards for Unwanted Behavior

If you remember "Jumpy" from chapter one, then you know this rule. Suppose you want Fido to sit. Instead he jumps on you to get you to play. Remove your attention. Just stand silently and as still as a tree. Keep your arms folded and look away. This tells Fido that what he's doing is not OK.

Rule 2: Reward Good Behavior Immediately

If Fido is performing the correct behavior, reward him within half a second. Yes, that's fast! Suppose Fido sits, but you reward him as he starts to get back up. You're actually rewarding him for getting up!

Rule 3: Focus on Your Movements

You read earlier that Fido doesn't understand most words. What he really cares about are your body language and his reward. Suppose Fido jumps on you and you shout "no." And you wave your arms to keep him away. He'll keep jumping. That's because your hand-waving makes you look just like a giant squeaky toy he wants to play with. So watch your movements and be consistent!

Rule 4: Use the Right Reward

Suppose Fido sits and you reward him with praise. But what he really wants is for you to toss him a ball or give him a treat. This will get Fido frustrated because he'll think you don't understand him. How do you know which reward to use? Study Fido and think: What would he rather have or be doing right now?

 **Tip** Food is one of the best rewards to use because your BFF has to eat. Be sure to check with your parents on what treats to use. To avoid giving Fido too many extra treats, it's best to take the food from his planned daily meals and use it for training. Just train around Fido's regular meal times.

Rule 5: Reward Every Time Until Fido Consistently Understands

At first, Fido may perform the correct behavior out of sheer luck. Want to make sure he knows what the correct behavior is? Reward him every time until he understands why he's getting a reward.

Rule 6: Train in Little Steps

Be patient and teach Fido step by step. Start with something easy and build up his skills. If you skip steps, Fido might not learn what you want him to do. And if you make Fido train for too long, he might get tired and bored. That's not good either.

Chapter 4
Training Time!

Got the rules down? Here are eight great activities for you and Fido. Remember to learn them in order!

Activity 1: The Automatic Sit

This trick will get Fido to "magically" sit.

STEP 3

1. Put five bite-size treats in your hand and make a fist.

2. Hold your hand near your belly button or higher. You want to keep the snacks way out of Fido's reach. (Far enough so he doesn't try to grab them!)

3. If he jumps to get it, stand up straight and be silent.

STEP 4

4. If you hold still and the treat looks tasty to Fido, he will sit.

5. The moment he sits—bam! Straighten your arm and put one treat into his mouth.

6. If he stays seated, give three or four additional treats. Make sure you stand up straight in between giving each of these treats. Also, pull your hand back to your body. This shows Fido that he's getting many individual treats.

STEP 5

7. Walk away quickly for several steps. Repeat this exercise when he follows you and then sits.

8. When Fido can do five to ten automatic sits in a row, go on to the next exercise.

22

Activity 2: Take Treats Nicely

Some dogs are so excited to get their treat, they grab. Teach Fido to be patient.

STEP 2

STEP 4

STEP 5

1. Start with Fido sitting or lying down. This way, he won't be moving around.

2. Put treats in your left hand. Then make a fist. Put this fist close to his face.

3. Hold your fist really still. He might sniff, lick, or gnaw at your hand.

4. Hold a second treat in your right hand. Then place it at your forehead. This treat will help lure Fido to look away from your fist and at your face. If he doesn't, wave this treat to get his attention.

5. When Fido moves his head away to look at your right hand, open your left hand wide, immediately! Give him the treat.

6. Repeat this exercise five to ten times in a row. After a while, he'll start to look up immediately when you show him your closed fist. At this point, you won't even need to use the treat in your right hand as a lure.

7. Once Fido understands this exercise, you (and your friends) should always give him treats this way. Only open your fist when he has shown patience by looking up.

Tip

Does your BFF have trouble sitting? If he just stands and stares at you for over 30 seconds, you can lure him to sit. Put a treat up to his nose and then draw it over his head so that he has to look up and lean back into a sit position.

23

Activity 3: Red Light, Green Light

This game trains Fido to follow you and then automatically sit whenever you stop.

STEP 2

STEP 3

STEP 4

1. Have Fido do an automatic sit. (Remember activity one?)

2. Next, run away from him in a straight line for just three to ten steps. Run fast enough so that he chases you.

3. Before he catches up to you, come to a screeching halt and turn to face Fido. Then stand still like a tree.

4. Reward Fido when he sits. As with the automatic sit, no commands!

5. Keep practicing by repeating the steps. Build up to cheering and sounding excited when you run. Fido will love playing this game and will get his exercise, too!

Tip If you run really fast in step 2, Fido might get overexcited. He might jump after he catches up to you in step 3. Be sure to start at a slower speed so he stays calm. Gradually up your running speed and distance. Over time, Fido will learn to automatic sit—even when he's superexcited!

Activity 4: Take Fido for a Walk

Time to take Fido for a walk on a leash! This activity builds on Red Light, Green Light on page 24. It teaches Fido to walk nicely beside you.

STEP 1

1. Start by choosing a side that you will stick with and have him sit on that side. Then speed-walk for five to ten steps. Make sure Fido is following and looking at you. Don't let Fido run past you! Then suddenly stop walking before he gets ahead of you.

STEP 2

2. Turn to face Fido slightly so that he will stop and sit by your side.

3. Reward him with one to three treats once he sits.

4. Repeat steps one to three a bunch of times. But vary the distance of your speed-walk.

STEP 3

5. You can even reward Fido while he's walking next to your side.

6. If Fido's front feet start to get ahead of yours, stop. He'll get to the end of the leash and then eventually sit and look at you. Reward him when he does this. Then start your walk again.

STEP 4

7. Practice consistently and Fido will be able to walk nicely next to you on a leash!

Activity 5: Sit Pretty and Beg

This activity is divided into three parts. That's because it can be a bit tricky for Fido. He has to learn how to balance first. Don't expect him to sit straight up in the beginning.

Part 1: The Basics

STEP 2

STEP 3

1. Have Fido sit on a nonslip surface. Hold several bite-size treats in one hand.

2. Take one treat with your other hand and put it up to Fido's nose. As he goes to sniff it, raise your hand. Be sure to keep the treat at his nose.

3. Did he follow the treat by lifting his front legs off the ground? If so, give him a treat. Make sure he gets it while his legs are still off the ground. If not, try positioning the treat a little differently.

4. Repeat part one until Fido can consistently balance with legs slightly off the ground. Once Fido aces this, move on to part two.

Part 2: Aim Higher

STEP 2

1. Repeat part one. But this time, raise your hand a little bit higher. Keep practicing until Fido can balance with two legs high off the ground.

2. Then raise your hand even higher. But not so high that he starts to stand. Continue practicing.

3. Once Fido manages this, aim higher. As soon as Fido can balance while sitting straight up, move on to step four.

4. You'll now train him to stay in this "beg position." Once he hits his mark, give him three to five treats in a row. Be sure to give the treats in a way that will help him stay in position.

5. For the first few practices, deliver the treats quickly. As Fido gets the hang of this activity, space out the treats. This way, Fido will learn to stay in position longer.

YAY!

STEP 4

Part 3: Add the Cue

1. When Fido can beg and balance consistently, prepare to teach him the cue word.

2. Start by holding completely still so that Fido will focus on the cue, not your movement.

SIT PRETTY!

STEP 3

3. Then say "Beg" or "Sit pretty" and follow by luring him into position with a treat.

4. If you can do this properly for twenty to thirty times in a row, Fido will start sitting pretty on cue. Eventually he won't even need you to lure him with food.

YAY!

STEP 4

Activity 6: Ride a Skateboard

Love your skateboard? Teach Fido to ride it and have some fun, too! This trick is for dogs with healthy knees and hips. Be sure to check with your parents to make sure that Fido is in the right shape to do this. Also, be safe! Ride only on a level location like a driveway or a playground. Do not ride on the street!

Part 1: Pre-boarding Exercise

STEP 1

1. Find a large, raised surface. This surface should be much larger than a skateboard. Objects you can use include a platform or several large books placed side by side. You can also use a wide piece of wood.

2. Once you've found it, put it on the ground. Then use treats to lure Fido toward it. When he places his front feet on the object, give him five to ten treats in a row.

YAY!

STEP 2

3. Then walk away so he gets off and follows you. (You can also toss a treat on the floor to get him to move.)

4. Repeat steps one to three until Fido can step on the object without hesitation five times in a row. (If Fido gets all four paws on the object, you can reward him, too.)

5. Next, walk up to the object without luring Fido with a treat. See if he steps on it. If he does, reward him. (If he gets all the way up the board, reward him, too.) Give him three to five more treats to get him to keep his front feet on the platform a bit longer.

LOOK AT ME!

STEP 5

6. When Fido has mastered step five, have him practice standing on a smaller board. Use something similar in size to a skateboard. At this stage he should automatically be running over to step on the board. He should be able to do it without a lure and even getting on.

Part 2: Get on Board!

1. Time to switch to an actual skateboard! In the beginning, make sure the skateboard doesn't move. You don't want to scare Fido. Try placing the board on grass or a thick carpet.

2. Just like in part one, lure Fido onto the board with treats and then go through the steps you took to get him to stand on a stationary board.

3. Is Fido comfortable standing on the board? OK, let's get the skateboard moving!

4. Put the skateboard on a smooth surface and let Fido step on it. When Fido can comfortably run and place his front legs on the skateboard to get it moving, he can ride it! When he's very excited, he'll jump on the board with all four feet! (Note: If your BFF is not excited about doing this kind of trick, don't push him!)

5. Practice this trick in sessions of five to fifteen minutes several times a day. In just several days, Fido may be a skate-boarding pro!

STEP 2

STEP 4

Activity 7: Leave It

Teach Fido to leave things he's sniffing or about to pick up. This includes your toys or food you dropped on the floor.

STEP 2

STEP 4

FREE!

YAY!

STEP 6

1. Hold a treat in your hand and have Fido stand in front of you.

2. Let him see the treat. Then drop it behind you.

3. When Fido moves forward to try to get to it, block him! Step in just like you're doing a basketball block. (Don't stop Fido by grabbing his leash. That would be cheating!)

4. If you stand still after you've successfully blocked him, he will do an automatic sit. Reward him with a treat.

5. Then give him a series of treats if he remains seated. Just like in activity one, remember to stand up straight in between treats.

6. Once he can look at you for two seconds straight, tell him "Free." At the same time, point to the treat you dropped earlier. Let him get his reward.

7. Keep practicing. Once you know that Fido will sit as soon as you block him, you can move on to step eight.

8. Say "Leave it" right before you toss the treat in step two. Pretty soon Fido will know what the cue word means. He'll get his smelly nose off things he finds. Rather than feeling deprived, he'll rush to you in case you might feel like giving him something better.

Activity 8: Play Bow

Now for the grand finale! Let's train Fido to take a bow for a job well done.

STEP 1

STEP 3

STEP 4

1. Put a treat right up to Fido's nose. Then lower it to the ground between his legs.

2. Push the treat back toward his chest. This will lead Fido to shift his weight toward his rear.

3. When his weight is on his back legs and his head is really low, reward him. Give him a series of treats for being in this odd position.

4. After a while, Fido will realize this: It would be easier for him to rest on his elbows in order to get the treats. Give him five treats in a row as he takes on this "play bow" position.

5. Keep practicing. Once Fido can strike the bow position every time you place a treat up to his face and then down low, move on to step six.

6. Hold completely still. Then add the cue words "play bow" an instant before you lure him with the treat in step one. Practice a bunch of times.

7. When you think Fido knows the cue, test him. Say "play bow." Then wait to see if he automatically does it!

Tip

Training activities can be tiring for Fido, especially if he has to think hard. Be sure to take short breaks from time to time.

Working with Dogs

You might be having so much fun with Fido that you are wondering how I got my job. Or how you might get my job someday. So, here's my story....

When I was a kid, I loved animals so much that I decided I'd become a veterinarian. Then, after many years of hard work, I graduated from veterinary school.

I started seeing animal patients. Everything was great at first. But then I realized that more pets were coming in with behavior problems than medical ones. This made me sad. I had worked through major behavior problems with my first dog, Max. I remembered how frustrating this was for both Max and me for his entire eleven-year life.

I thought: How could I help my clients so that they could be more successful with their pets? I went back to school to study for a master's degree in animal behavior. During that time, I studied how dogs communicated through barking. I also worked on projects in which I trained horses, giraffes, ostriches, and even chickens! Can you believe that?

If only I had known then what I know now, Max and I could have solved our problems in just a few weeks. We could have had more fun together!

Luckily, now I can help my animal patients and their families. And I can share what I've learned with you. Then you'll be able to really understand your BFF and make the most of your friendship with your dog!

You can learn more about my work at www.drsophiayin.com.